Did Martin Luther go on a Diet of Worms?

Did Martin Luther Go On a Diet of Worms?
Text and Illustration Copyright: by Thuy Vu
Published: August 2014

ISBN-13: 978-1500815813
ISBN-10: 1500815810

Did Martin Luther
go on a
Diet of Worms?

Thuy Vu

Did Martin Luther
go on a diet of worms?
Did he eat them?
Those squishy,
mushy,
vermin crawling with germs?

Or was it something else?
Read on and see
if this "Diet of Worms"
is what it appears to be.

This baby is Martin Luther.
He was born in Germany
on November the 10th,
1483.

His dad worked in mining.
His mom had eight kids in all.
He easily excelled at school
and in college he studied Law.

One day on Luther's way home
a lightning bolt struck so closely,
that to Saint Anna he cried,
(since he nearly died),
that if he lived, a monk he would be!

As a monk he prayed and worked hard;
he fasted and confessed.
But then he would learn
that God's love is not earned
but could be freely possessed!

It was that blessed day when
he read Romans chapter one:

"THE RIGHTEOUS SHALL LIVE BY FAITH."

Man is saved by grace alone!

The church instead said differently
and sent indulgences to sell.
"All you'll need is a coin or two
to make a lost soul well."

To dispute those foul practices,
in 1517
he hammered the 95 Theses
to a church door on Halloween.

The invention of the printing press
dispersed the information.
His writing went
throughout Germany
and sparked the Reformation.

At the Diet of Worms
he was threatened punishment
if he did not recant.

But he could not go against
conscience nor scripture
so he firmly held his stance.

and "Worms" was the city
where Luther would be called to defend:
the 95 Theses,
all his treatises,
and the rest of the
works he had penned.

He later wrote many hymns,
and the Bible he would also translate.

Thankfully history would show,
that as far as we know –

There were never any worms
on his plate!

I'll trust in God's unchanging Word
Till soul and body sever,
For, though all things shall pass away,
His Word shall stand forever!

Martin Luther

Made in United States
North Haven, CT
02 October 2023